Into The Mind
A Sampling of a Poet

Laura Olson

Copyright © 2012 Laura Olson
Witcher Mountain
All rights reserved.
ISBN-13: 978-0615673431

DEDICATION

To my husband, my partner
in life.
And to my parents, who never gave
up on me.

Table of Contents

Into The Mind

Night's Playground	3
Metal Wings	4
Keys	5
Faces	6
Water Inhaled	8
Fear	9
The Final Hour	10
Waiting	12
Words	14
A Painting	16
On Paper	18
No Answer	19
We Teach	20
Finding the Lost Child	21
The Voices	22

Lucks Paradox

Altered	25
Broken	26
Fate's Secret	27
It Is So	28
Luck's Paradox	30
Shattered Hourglass	32
Injustice Won	34
Road Trip	35
The Cry	36
When the End Came	37

Love Bits

Be	38
Know My Heart	39

Ashes	40
Branches	41
La Esperanza	42
Carry On	43
Amour	44
Loneliness	45

Nature's Gift

Days	47
Time	48
I Kin Ye	49
Rugged Old Horse	50
Puffin	51
The Hunt	52
The Change	54
Tomorrow	55
Woodland Night	56
Young Ones	57

Under The Sheets

Beat of Life	59
Complete	60
Locked away	61
One	62
Lust	64
Desire	65
Midnight	66

Into The Mind

Laura Olson

I have many different faces, always changing in time. I reflect images of the world around me. Some animated and full of motion, others lifeless and still.

I have acquired many stories to tell. Creations from the mind. An imagined biography told by the ones who look at me. Tales of inner worlds and luck, gone bad.

The other side, if you step inside of my world. Another like me, telling the true beauty, the fairest of all. A crack, a break, not one, but seven.

I am fragile, easy to destroy. An injury shatters images into a kaleidoscope of colors. My views become distorted. I lose my ability to portray reality and truth.

A still, dark room. Everything left in its lifeless state. Hair a mess, mascara running down flushed cheeks, tears wetting the skin, dripping off the nose onto blue carpet. A kitten hissing, arching its back at the identical twin in front of it.

Join me…

Night's Playground

The mind is a playground
fear the favorite toy
for the encompassing darkness
closing in all around
The suffocation of light
desperate to escape
bringing the shadows alive
to frolic in the night
Creatures of the black
come out from hiding
never to be seen
always behind the back
Throwing out clues
to trigger insane thoughts
the imagination goes wild
with threats of new

Laura Olson

Metal Wings

Under the wings, cutting through the dark
the red glow, the heartbeat in the sky.
Air lifts and supports, defying gravity
consorting with the metal bird, above the clouds.

Under the fluff of white pillows, floating
on their way, mingling into blankets
blocking the glitter of lights scattered
in the blackness below.

Under the lights, glowing majestically
with power, chasing away blindness
from the eyes, searching around corners
unknown, exploring.

Under the eyes, looking at thoughts
as they interact in the minds sanctuary
feeding the dreams of creation, the birth
of metal wings.

Into The Mind

Keys

Shades of shine
Pointed array
Jagged yet smooth
Each individual
Bringing to life
Locking away
Attached to the circles
Of diversity
Never ending
A purpose in curves
Points, sharp edges
Lines of direction
Telling a story
An autobiography
Remembering travels
Leading
To the individual
Keeper of keys

Laura Olson

Faces

Faces in the blood,
dark red, hot,
a fresh wound.
Soul deep,
that cannot heal.
More pain than
anyone can feel.
A heart ripped
out, from inside.
Now empty
of life, draining
out, to nothing,
Overwhelmed, the stain
of guilt.
A mind torn
between personalities.
Different personalities,
but the same.
The paradox of want,
faces left to haunt.
The clock of life
tick, ticks away,
not to go back
but remembers,
never to forget
a sin, guilt
and blame reside
searching
for a reasonable cause.
Always finding
but never hiding,
growing among the sins
of the past.
A tear waiting to fall

Into The Mind

but trapped
without life.
It hovers,
wanting to be relieved.
It will always be there,
on the edge,
like the edge of sanity
coming near.
Sins of the naive one
who worships
the wrong two.
From a different world,
all three from the same
pearl. In disguise,
not real.
Like a play
put on stage
for the pleasure
of another.
Only hurting those
who perform.
The act of happiness,
what is right.
Robotic movements of bribery,
all done for love
and approval,
that is never real.
Reality becomes nonexistent,
turning into a nightmare.
The haunted honeymoon.
Haunted by ghosts
deep inside.

Laura Olson

Water Inhaled

Stars talking,
words unheard
by the ear.
But heard
by the eyes.
Eyes feeling
their way
through darkness.
The only light,
punctures, down
into the skin.
Pricking holes
deep inside.
The blue sky
suffocating lungs
as it flows, down
the throat
into the body.
Like cold
water inhaled.
Looking at
wind, as it
passes, the clouds.
Across the sky,
the clouds
muffle whispers
from the moon,
coloring thoughts.

Fear

Helplessness, feeling
alone. Hunger.
The unexplained,
no power.
Responsibility
growing, trying
today, fighting
yesterday, resisting
tomorrow. Being
yourself. Success,
failure. Being
loved. Trusting,
giving, accepting.
Owning anger.
Giving up,
giving in.
Taking in
tomorrow
Temporary.

Laura Olson

The Final Hour

Never ending
obsessions, overtake
the mind. Seeping
into the soul, creeping
from behind.
No elimination,
this unbearable possession
hangs around, waiting
to teach.
Heart turns to stone,
callas and cold.
No emotion left, nothing
to be told.
Desire for revenge, appears
in fantasies, eventually
breaking, into reality, slowly
finding the key.
Anger bubbles up
to the surface,
the witch's concoction
casting an evil spell
as it comes
from the cauldron.
Ticking, a clock
minutes into hours, desperate,
trying to turn back, unable
to stop, it's powers.
The final hour,
to come
not knowing, negative
forces surround, no
resistance, to bend.
Only time can release,
from evil's stalking

Into The Mind

torture, lurking
in dark shadows,
deep, the mind unsure.

Laura Olson

Waiting

Heavy clouds hang
like a pillow filled
with ice. Coldness
seeps though
colder as it falls.

Sunlight unable
to penetrate
this mass of darkness.
It waits, on top
to find it's chance.

Time never stopping
its journey, an immortal
being, breathing away
seconds, minutes, hours,
days, months.

Mortal ones trapped
underneath, waiting
for the day, the sun
peeks through. This ceiling,
the prison cell.

Leaves of fall turn
colors, drying up.
Their beauty blowing
as they die, leaving
branches, cold and bare.

Is this the forever
that never ends?
A season that comes
to change? Will the sunlight

Into The Mind

come again, brilliant?

Laura Olson

Words

Words rush in,
that's all they are.
Words, words, words.
No meaning held.
Just something to say
to break the silence,
unbearable silence.
The aftermath,
when words
become words.
Not like the past,
when words
were everything.
One word said all,
what was to come.
A word meant to say
all emotions in one.
Now they are empty
of feelings.
Nothing left to trust.
Words to words,
day to day,
when there's nothing
but useless words.
No beginning or end.
Empty of matter,
empty of life.
Just filling the time,
draining the mind.
Reminding of dreams,
those unfinished dreams.
Emotions hidden away
released once with words.
Instead are the words

Into The Mind

of nothing, lacking all feeling.
Words passing through
a mechanical expression.
Programmed, nothing behind
or in them at all.
A world full of nothing
but words, words, words.

Laura Olson

A Painting

The mind of an artisan
on canvas.

Paper
jumps from two dimensions
to three.

Illusion of a sixth sense
in a reality with only five.

The past,
the future,
the present,
together one time
in a painting.

A painting
bringing out senses
unknown.

On the wall:
The presentation.

A homemade
snapshot
of memory.

The unfamiliar
brought to the familiar,
paint.

A discovery,
history
brought through the ages.

Into The Mind

Each painting,
a puzzle piece from the past.

Laura Olson

On Paper

Let it out
Bursting
Like a balloon
So full of pressure
It needs a release
Write it down
On paper
Show the feelings
Using only words
Put on paper
Describe every emotion
Let it all flow
Like water
Or maybe tears
Tears put on paper
Don't lock it inside
Destroying the promise
Of beauty
Turn to the heart
Put it on paper
A heart so full
Once angry
Filled with aggression
Or maybe devastation
Broken into pieces
Healed with happiness
But scarred eternal
Put it on paper
The therapeutic art
Creation through feelings
Emotions needing to escape
Through the ink of a pen
Put on to paper

No Answer

Knocking on the door
Waiting for an answer
Wanting to get in
Reaching inside
Trying to grasp
Something
Unable to get through
Calling out names
Sending a message
No one hears
Or maybe they ignore
Pushing it aside
Until tomorrow
Where nothing else
Can get in the way
If tomorrow comes
Dodging the arrows
Stalling for time
The time needed
For other things
Dealing with too much
Alone, on their own
Full of fear
Of what is to come
What fate might bring
If they don't answer
Or if they do

Laura Olson

We Teach

With our hands, we support
budding dreams of potential.

With our minds, we create
experiences to remember.

With our words, we influence
hope for the possible.

With our knowledge, we share
opportunities for the future.

With our hearts, we nurture
the sprouts of tomorrow.

Finding the Lost Child

Did you ever wonder
What secrets lie deep inside
Minds that have shut down
Thoughts untapped, pushed aside

The child who looks away
Shows no interest in tomorrow
Have they been forgotten
Left with their spirit unheard

Have you ever listened
For the song never sung
The story locked within
Understanding sparked by fun

Did you ever look
At the beauty of knowledge
Dancing of words onto paper
Movements of body and mind

Have you ever opened
Gifts brought to you each day
Searching for connections
With lessons explored

Have you watched a mind engage
Intelligence of many colors
The style of creativity
Process leading the way

Nurturing creative thought
Opportunities to explore
Shaping foundations
Experiences of the mind

Laura Olson

The Voices

I can hear the familiar voices of loved ones all around me. I recognize their touch, as one by one, I feel a kiss on the cheek or a hand holding mine. I can't move my hand, though, as hard as I try. I can feel wetness on the cheeks of those who get close. The moisture that escapes into my mouth reveals tears. I can taste the salty liquid. People are crying. I don't know why. I try to ask, but my mouth won't move. The words are trapped, inside.

I can smell my husband's cologne, the strong scent lingers in the air. I can feel blankets covering my body. I'm lying down, it feels like a bed. I can still hear voices, but they fade in and out like a faraway radio station. I try to focus on what they're saying, catching only a few words at a time. I hope to figure out where I am.

My eyes, useless to reality, only see what my mind conjures up. In my mind, I see the figures of those around me, foggy and distorted. I feel as if I'm trapped in a dream unable to control my body. At times, I feel like I'm floating in a make-believe world. The visions in my mind spinning into swirls of light. A pleasant fragrance of wildflowers fills my nose. I get the feeling of peaceful serenity. I'm drawn to the light.

I still hear voices. They echo through my mind. I feel them pulling me away from the light. They're crying out to me. Memories of my past flash into my mind. Every sense is aroused and it seems like I'm reliving past events.

My dream world and reality hold on to me, each one coaxing me to join them. I have to choose. The calm, relaxing sensation from the bright light is almost addicting. One look and you want to venture towards it. The curiosity, overwhelming. At the same time, each step to take me farther from reality. The voices become muffled and harder to hear. Although I feel no fear of what's ahead, I sense if I go too far, there's no return.

Then I hear a voice. It's my little girl, only three years old. I can smell the baby lotion on her soft skin. I make out the word mommy, as it escapes from her innocent mouth. I feel pain as I think of leaving the world she is in. I try to block out the light and the sensual feelings it sends with its rays. The voices become louder and clearer. I begin to taste the stale air. My mouth is dry. The light begins to fade into darkness. I feel my husband's hand around mine. I try to squeeze it and it works. With everything inside, I try to open my eyes. I can feel my eyelashes as my eye's flutter open. I instantly squint as the outside light shines in. I look around as everyone smiles and watches me. A hospital room. Very white, very stuffy, but real.

Laura Olson

Lucks Paradox

Into The Mind

Altered

Shattered bones, hijacked dreams,
promises stolen, as metal
makes contact with flesh. The first
weapon of influence, alcohol
mixed, with wheels and headlights.
A deadly creation of Mr. Hyde.

The passion of the sky, now
taken. Broken futures.
A fork in the trail of life divides
thoughts of time escaping, the lost
year. Adding time to the body,
to the mind. Hope fades

into the pavement. Fate slithers in
bringing change, perceptions
of opportunities stolen.
Independence becomes shaky, pain
moves in and stays, becoming everything
for all the days and more.

Borrowing from sleep, creating
the nightmare that
attaches like the baby clinging
to its mother, primal.
Snapshots of the present, rob
snapshots of the future. Dreams

altered, by metal and pavement,
wheels and headlights and yet no one
responsible, for the crime.
The destruction of a body,
a son, a sister, a father, a mother
now starting again, altered.

Laura Olson

Broken

Broken feet, crumbled,
smoldering charcoal,
black, blueishly hot
glowing embers swollen.
Random misshapen
cuts, breaking smooth
dignified skin.

Bubbles of pain travel,
tubes of red, blood
stained, become you
entering the chest.
Lungs emptying
a broken cage,
protection weakened.

Your eyes, a look
never seen, beyond
life. Holding the sight,
the smile, colliding
with life. Seconds
a life is gone, two broken
left with wires and questions.

Fate's Secret

There was an angel with them that day
breathing the life back into their bodies
crushed by impact and air. At the mercy
of Fate. Twisted metal, sculptured
by speed and force, surrounded
their now frail bodies. Glass sprinkled
amidst the blood. The angel held
their hearts in her hand gently,
with just enough love to push
life's liquid throughout, keeping
the flow of survival. Only the angel
knows the secret of Fate and why
they weren't taken, on that wet
highway, as tears fell from the heavy
clouds onto the pavement.

Laura Olson

It Is So

Have you ever felt
Like giving up
Why bother, is it not
Already planned
Predestined, if God
Has made it,
It is so
Right

Questions, is it
My fault, should
I believe more or
Why bother, no
One knows for sure
Although
They'll tell you
It is so
Right

Does it make
A difference
Is it luck, maybe
Fate, a master plan
Who decides, who divides
It up, why is fair
In the dictionary
That plan, you know
It is so
Right

Struggle, pain, challenge
So you can leave
It to someone
Else, give the control

Into The Mind

Mold the future, ripped goals
More blame, who's
Fault, in the eyes
Of the decider
That predestined
Shit
It is so
Right

He only gives
What you can handle
Even if you die
Trying
Even if you try
Dying
Won't help, just
Guilt, damned
If you do, damned
If you don't
It is so
Right

It comes down
To money, you
Crave it? No
Just need it
To be, to make it
To do it
Right, to be
Good
It is so
Right

Laura Olson

Luck's Paradox

Lucky the engine dropped
below, breaking your feet
not your spine.

Lucky the airbags crushed
ribs and spleens
not your mind.

Lucky the seatbelt scarred,
taking the breath from within,
keeping you safe inside.

Lucky the windshield shattered,
glass in saran wrap, stayed
less in your face.

Lucky for the two ton truck crushed
around the cab you were in
not a car flattened.

Lucky for the jaws ripping,
cutting open metal, prying
freedom with pain.

Lucky the hood crumbled,
like paper, creased in front
rather than through.

Lucky for the hat,
five minute, five thousand dollar hat,
flight for life's souvenir.

Lucky it was him
alcohol creates his eulogy

Into The Mind

thankful it wasn't you.

Luck's paradox granted you
pain and suffering, fragile life
rather than death's welcome.

I'll take Luck's Paradox
to see you recover, survive
come out alive, come home.

Laura Olson

Shattered Hourglass

One life
falling apart
waiting to break
when it hits
shattering
like an hourglass
time escapes
the sand
still runs out
out of it's place
into the new
what to do
nothing
but one
pick up the pieces
solve the puzzle
save the time
build from scratch
a new hourglass
another life.

Into The Mind

Injustice Won

I never understood
why one
so sure of hatred
towards his people
turns around
giving reason
for this hate.
Everyone together
must be equal
when this one speaks
of his people
he separates
segregates.
One group singles
themselves out
fights violence
with violence,
discrimination
with discrimination.
The innocent hurt
the guilty watch.
No justice done,
injustice won.

Laura Olson

Road Trip

Black, as far as the eye can see.
Headlights creeping out
chasing the darkness
as it escapes.
Neon moon beating
to mile markers
counting down time.
Lines shooting
underneath, immersed
in the rhythm
of the road.
Slap happy giggles in
the backseat.
Sound of the wind,
gliding down, meeting
the sides of the car.
Lights dotting the distance.
Sleeping shadows
pass quickly.

The Cry

Eyes of torture, looking,
true unbearable pain,
stop the pain. Imminent
cry of remarkable
pain, wanting to die.
End the pain, another
cry, help. Doctors around
not stopping, consuming
pain. Don't touch me,
you cry, I try, reassurance
but why, stop the pain.
A talented pill, waiting
for what, results
confirmation, mastered
pain, reaching out, taking
hold of thoughts.
Bringing, smothering
giving insanity, pain
surrounding the cry
immobized within.
Take the pain, contain
feed it drugs, perfect
relief withheld, to come.
The cry, give me
something, take me,
no more pain.

Laura Olson

When the End Came

Everything was so clear
at one point, a life
mapped out with dreams, following
a straight line.
Hope, of what was
to come, a heart
without fear, so willing
to succumb. Powerful,
controlling the mind,
despite looming danger
eyes become blind. Words
become useless
from those who advised
making them enemies, more
despised. When the end
came, dropped like a bomb.
Exploding, tearing into
the calm, emotion
turned evil, anger built
up, replacing love
until it could subside.
Not disappearing, hiding
somewhere deep
in the soul
a smoldering fire
burning coals. Time leads
bitterness, lost faith,
a strong sense of caution
always watching.

Into The Mind

Love Bits

Laura Olson

Be

Be
you, love
yourself, find
light, the burn.
Reach
for tomorrow.
Embrace
memories.

Be
happy, know
beauty within.
Hold
my heart,
gently, keep it
with you.
Love.

Be
content, peace
inside, feel.
Breathe
life, my breath
to yours. Take
part of me,
Safe.

Be

Know My Heart

Know my heart
Feels every joy
Each success
Held dear
Your smile
Pumps through
Failures grasp
Deep inside
All the pain
I take on
Sadness consumes
Builds strength
For tomorrow
Keep with you
All my heart

Laura Olson

Ashes

Time and time
again, I sit
and think.
You and I, love
left behind,
once raging
like a fire
melting hearts.
But a flame, hot,
sometimes burns
to nothing, but
ashes, turning
cold and grey.
Drifting darkness, leaving
memories trapped,
inside ashes,
yearning.

Branches

I need you,
as a seed
needs water
to grow
to sprout, escaping
from inside.
Love growing
stronger, thirstier
reaching beyond,
nourishing life.
A trunk, a base
to support,
to continue.
Our life
branches out
different directions,
the trunk stays
holding the branches
keeping them steady
giving freedom
to wander
to grow
to change.

Laura Olson

La Esperanza

El domino, slips
half reaching, grasping
desperado, to hold on.
Not knowing, what
to come, if you let go.
The other, enamorarse
deeper, the unknown.
Afraid if you hit
bottom, everything
destrozar, or is there
an end. Maybe
para siempre.
Never feel the pain
when it stops, solamente
again. The past continues,
preoccupying thoughts,
reminding, buried peccadilloes.
Never allowed to discard,
a broken world
before. Now coming
juntamente, cut like a jigsaw,
everything left
won't rip apart.
La esperanza.

Carry On

Time brought us back
together, in the end.
Two roads crossed,
paths of destiny
only merging.

Life's cruelties provide
a link, common.
A chance to take,
put back pieces,
broken lives, bringing.

Memories rush
back, filling voids.
Time spent. Existence
arouses, strong feelings
afore laid to rest.

Innocence taken,
freedom gone.
A world, before us.
Responsibility, never
to go back.

You and I, remember
shared thoughts, bonds
lost. Yet found.
Verses never told.
Carry on, endure.

Laura Olson

Amour

Love was pretty,
so pretty. Dreams
and desires. All
falling into place.

Love powered
vows, for better
or worse. You
don't think worse.

Love, no fairytale.
But strong, binding
souls. Connecting
systems, minds.

Love surpasses, beauty
by eyes, conquers
words heard, challenges
thoughts, solidifies.

Love becomes you.
Merge, grows one.
Shelters, supports, feels
cries, with you.

Love idles, waiting
to brace, lifting.
Providing life, keeping
home, ready.

Into The Mind

Loneliness

    a flockless bird
    an abandoned child
    a single snowflake
    an empty heart

Laura Olson

Nature's Gift

Days

Days
dreary, cold, covered in
snow

Turning
flowers growing in the
sun

Rising
heat beats down on the
ground

Falling
leaves flutter from the
branches

Life
the changing seasons of
time

Laura Olson

Time

The cool breeze blew through
her hair, as dark as coal, standing
out amongst the autumn colors
behind her hands, holding a cold
glass. The leaves began to transform

into splatters of color, as if
on a canvas. The apples, bold,
begin their ripened descent
from the shadows of the leaves, asking
to be collected. Fallen memories

flutter through her mind like leaves
searching for the ground. Birds
sing of their departure, follow
the one before on the journey away
welcoming, the chill in the air, biting

noses and fingertips that have yet
to seek shelter in the fabric
of life. Of history unnoticed
in hands that create shelter
from the cold's craving of skin

that ages with loving detail.
Time continues on, leaving the warmth
of the season past, in the memories
of those who hold the clock
ensuring time's existence.

For what would time be if no one
was here to keep it?

I Kin Ye

I kin ye
Love and understand
Come with me
Let me take your hand

I will show you
Teach the Cherokee way
We can sit and watch
The morning birth of the day

The glow of life
Awakening all around
Engaging the spirit mind
Listening to the sounds

Find your secret place
Learn as ye go
Walk the road ahead
Only you will know

Follow the Spring Branch
Where it may go
And never forget
The home that you know

Father Mountain watches over
Mother Nature our friend
Look for the truth
It will be there in the end

Laura Olson

Rugged Old Horse

Tattered mane embracing, your strong neck,
the color of snow, melting just enough
for the earth underneath to loan
it's shades. I can see strength
rippling throughout your elder muscles,
toned and tried from experience. Tired eyes
holding the stories and sights from
long ago, justified respect. Like the child
looking into his grandfather's gentle eyes.
They tell of journeys to places unknown,
hooves quickly kissing the ground
moving on, moving on, moving on, swiftly
and gracefully. Time has followed
and finally reached you.

Puffin

What are you thinking
little bird? With sadness
radiating from those eyes
peeking out of your
burrowed sanctuary.
Crisp green leaves,
shades of white splattered
on top, extending the beauty
all around. A majestic
entrance to your humble
abode. Are you curious
about me, as we watch
one another, every tentative
movement, we absorb
tiny details, as if communicating
thoughts of wonder. Can we
share this gift, this Earth.

Laura Olson

The Hunt

I sit, I wait, patiently
the perfect moment
which all of me, attacks.
One swift motion, taking
my find, but, a brilliant
escape of this creature,
before my time came.
Off I search, something
to satisfy the need,
the rumbling inside me.
Quick, rhythmic strides
legs travel through
weeds, paws landing on
rough ground. My eyes, spy
the flow of water, softening
dirt as it goes. My ears, hear
peace. With the lap
of my tongue, I am overcome
refreshing feelings. To pause,
to rest, to ponder
where to continue, my quest
to heal the ache.
A sudden scent, familiar
stalking begins again. I see
opportunity, slowly creeping
towards my victim, eyes
never leaving it's path. Stop
to wait, prepare, plan
the attack. A quick pounce
leading to capture, assuring
continuing existence. Next
to find a place, to break.
The feasting ground, safety
shelter, myself never free,

Into The Mind

always on guard. For I
can become victim, prey
of my predator.

Laura Olson

The Change

Red, gold, orange erupt
The last dying flames of summer
Entering autumn

Flower of sunset
Reaching high into the sky
Before frost arrives

Drops of lavender
Moving in the cool breeze
Fading into fall

The floating leaves
Beginning a new journey
Touching the ground

Evergreens crawling
Across the tops of rocks
As if searching

Tomorrow

Wandering alone
Along its path
Never to stop
Never to look back
Itself immortal
Forever to live
Holding all sights
Past
Present
Future
Watching over
All knowing
Seeing every event
Traveling too fast
Traveling too slow
When boredom strikes
Free to do
Whatever
Free to control
Life.

Laura Olson

Woodland Night

Invisible sounds, escaping the dark
gray smoke, standing still.
An owl's question, as it sits, watching
the chatter of a raccoon, traveling
the flight of the bat, cutting through
silence. Shattered stillness.
The cry of the coyote, as it is looks
for something, in the dark.
Shadows creep through the mind. The crack
of a branch, whips the crisp air.
A cricket sings seduction to another.
The stream slides down rocks,
carrying messages of the spirits,
soothing the restless. Light dances
in the water, eyes of the forest.
Wind, playful in the trees.
Leaves whispering secrets, gossiping
frogs hide with the rocks. The moon
swallowed by clouds, stealing
the light, encouraging darkness
to keep the secrets.

Into The Mind

Young Ones

The sunlight outlines
the young bodies
glowing in the dawn
playful in the dew
in the morning light
one watching over
protecting, teaching

Laura Olson

Under the Sheets

Into The Mind

Beat of Life

Creases of satin
waves in the sheets
passion is alive
the primal echo
drawing two lovers
into one infinity
filling the heart
with love's mystery
undressing thoughts
and dreams carefully
deep into the night
a love only ending
with the last breath
the last beat of life.

Laura Olson

Complete

Limp shudders
Electric trickles
Throughout
Satisfaction yet
Yearning to stay
Never move from
The closeness
Sticky sweat, exhaustion,
Exhilaration, time
Wanders away
Reality released from
Private moments
Shared, only two
Intertwined as one
Skin to skin
Thought to thought
Lingering spasms crawl
Inside, escaping
Controlling, reliving
The moment together
Complete

Into The Mind

Locked away

Your eyes, draw me
closer, bringing feelings
to the surface.
They stay, patiently
waiting for time,
when they are free
to show you
feelings, so many
things to say, to do.

Laura Olson

One

You come, late
bringing need
to be close.

Into your eyes
drawing me,
revealing hunger.

I see, I'm
pulled in, shared
desires.

One touch, sending
shivers, crawling
along skin.

Lips meet
tender, feelings
engulf the mind.

Bodies pressed
together, touching
without shame.

Freedom, welcoming
nature, giving
pleasure.

Becoming one, knowing
nothing else
you and I.

Time stops, worlds
frozen, on our

Into The Mind

own, closer.

Laura Olson

Lust

A want so strong
It consumes your every thought
A dangerous addiction
Too powerful to be fought
A burning desire
Raging deep down inside
An uncontrollable craving
With the need to be satisfied
An evil possession
Always haunting the mind
Untamed feelings
Not to be left behind

Into The Mind

Desire

The storm inside
Raining down skin
Releasing the cry
Held deep within
Thoughts whisper
Misting the mind
Question the senses
With snaking time
I sense your shadow
Coming from behind
Wishing
To join

Laura Olson

Midnight

Total comfort
No control
Time defied
Midnight memories
Ecstasy alive
Beauty born
Fulfilled fantasies
Exotic pain
Seizures of lust
Other worlds
Safe escape
Treasures discovered
Love's art
Creation's seed
Sinful desire
Ecstatic need
Orgasmic tickles
Life

Appendix

My Translations
Spanish To English
From La Esperanza

El Domino - The Control
Desperado - Desperate
Enamorarse - To fall in love
Destrozar - To shatter
Para Siempre - Forever
Solamente - Alone
Peccadilloe - Small Sins
Juntamente - Together
La Esperanza - The Hope

Coming Soon…
Watch for the next collection of poems by Laura Olson.

Emovere: Energy In **Motion**

A collection of poems about the raw emotion and traumatic reality of being involved in the child protection system. An exploration into the perspectives of the children, the families and the professionals involved. Laura speaks from personal experience inside this world of emotional despair, instinct, passion and hope for tomorrow.

Thank you!

I am thankful for everyone who purchases my work and gives me one more opportunity to share my writing with others. My dream to yours....

Life's tomorrow is getting ***INTO THE MIND***.

www.ingramcontent.com/pod-product-compliance
Lightning Source LLC
Chambersburg PA
CBHW051712040426
42446CB00008B/853